This Book Belongs To

Notes